TopReaders

Beastly Bugs

Denise Ryan

Contents

What Is a Bug? 4

All Kinds of Bugs 6

Beetles 8

Butterflies 10

Spiders 12

Bees 14

Food 16

Flying 18

Swimming 20

Jumping 22

Quiz 24

There are all kinds of bugs
and some of them are beastly!
Let's find out about them.

What Is a Bug?

There are many kinds of bugs.
Insects, such as beetles, flies,
butterflies, bees, and ants,
are all bugs.

wing

Bees have six legs and
two pairs of wings.

wing

bee

head

leg

All Kinds of Bugs

There are more than a million kinds of insects. They live almost everywhere on Earth.

These flies can flap their wings and stay in the air a long time. They are called hover flies.

hover fly

Beetles

Some beetles cannot fly.
They have hard wings
that are joined together.

Hercules beetles

pincer

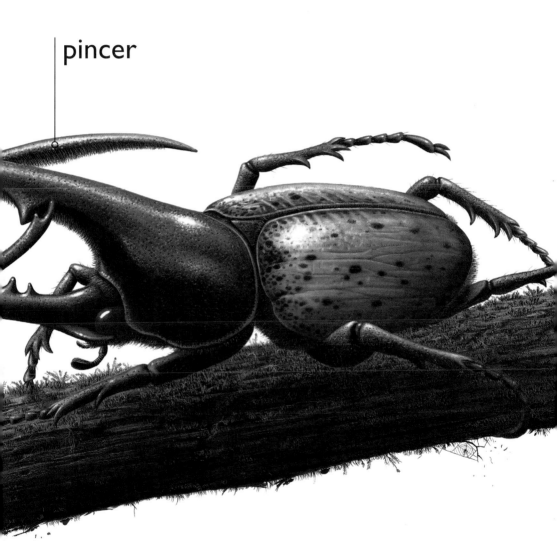

These Hercules beetles have pincers
at the front of their mouths.

Butterflies

Butterflies are beautiful flying insects. Baby butterflies are called caterpillars.

wing

butterfly

A butterfly has four large wings.

wing

wing

wing

Spiders

Spiders make a silky thread in their body. This is what their webs are made from.

Insects get trapped in the spider's web and the spider eats them.

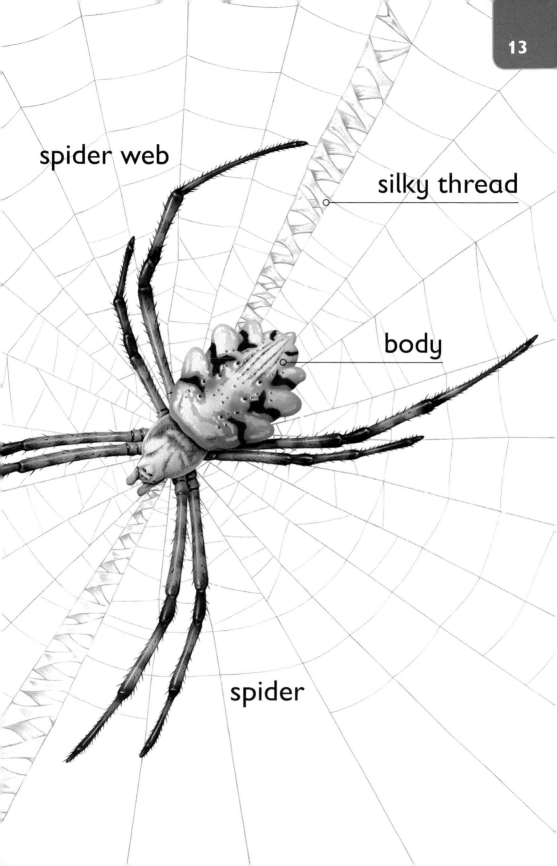

spider web

silky thread

body

spider

Bees

Bees live in honeycomb made from waxy cells. This is where they look after their young and store honey.

bee

honeycomb

waxy cell

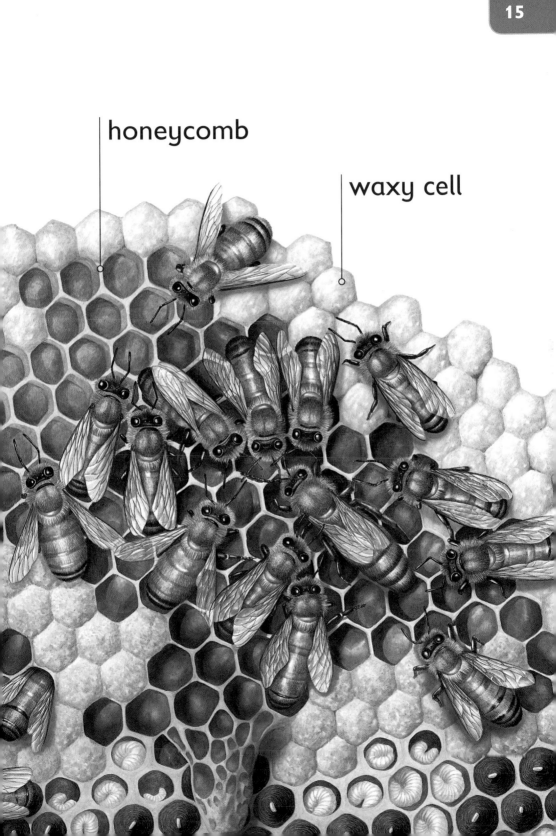

Food

Insects eat plants, seeds, fruit, small animals, and other insects.

butterfly

This praying mantis is eating a butterfly.

praying mantis

Flying

Most insects have one or two pairs of wings. They are good fliers.

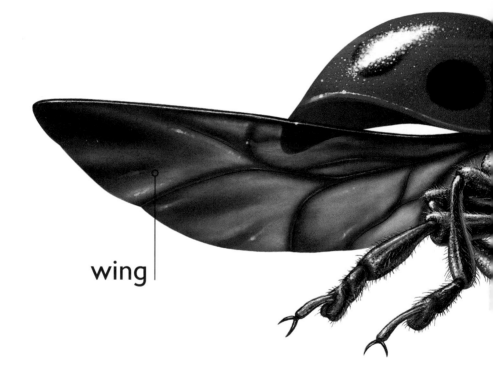

wing

Ladybugs are small insects. Their wing covers are red with black spots.

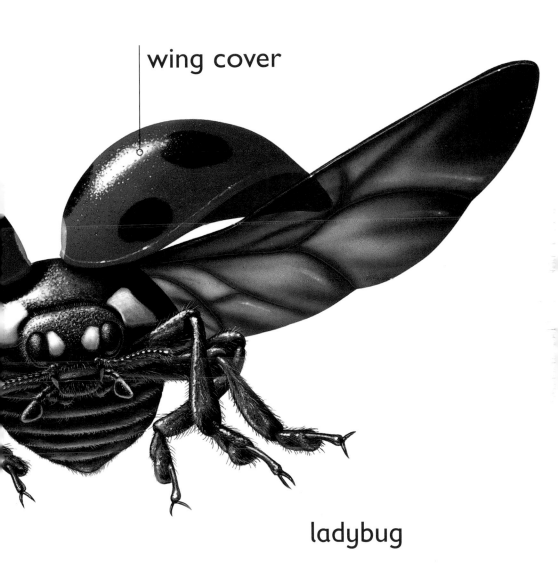

wing cover

ladybug

Swimming

Some insects can swim.
They swim in puddles,
pools, lakes, and rivers.

Some insects swim upside down.
They use their legs like oars.

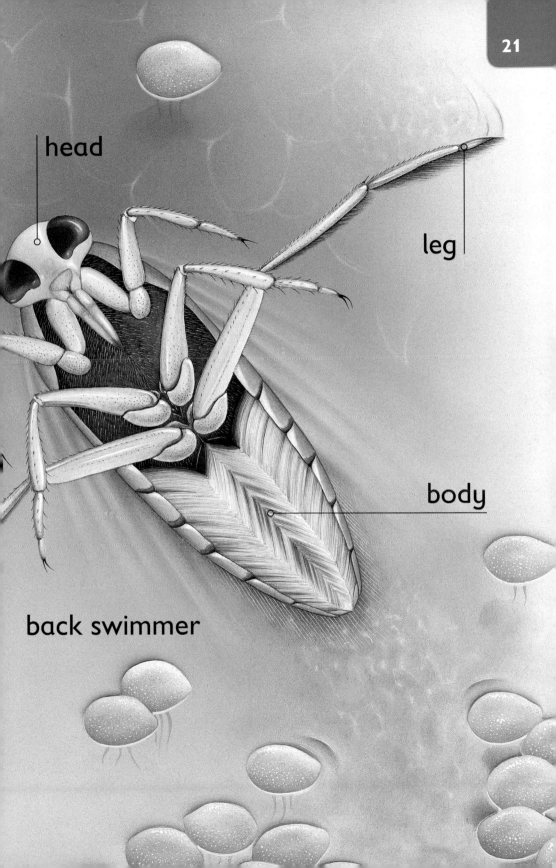

head

leg

body

back swimmer

Jumping

Some insects can jump.
Grasshoppers jump away
from their enemies.

strong leg

grasshopper

Grasshoppers have six legs with strong muscles.

Quiz

Can you match each bug
with its name?

butterfly

bee

ladybug

spider